LAST MAKINGS

Last Makings

POEMS BY

EARLE BIRNEY

M&S

Canadian Cataloguing in Publication Data

Birney, Earle, 1904–
    Last Makings

Poems.
ISBN 0-7710-1471-6

1. Love poetry, Canadian (English).* I. Title.

PS8503.I7L38 1991   C811'.54   C91-093084-8
PR9199.3.B58L38 1991

Typeset by The Typeworks, Vancouver.

Printed and bound in Canada

McClelland & Stewart Inc.
The Canadian Publishers
481 University Avenue
Toronto, Ontario   M5G 2E9

For Wailan Low
whose love and devotion made possible
the happiest years of my life

CONTENTS

Introduction

I've known Earle Birney since the early 1950s. A young genius named Curt Lang and I scraped acquaintance by writing provocative letters to him; and also to Edmund Wilson and Roy Campbell. I'd been reading Wilson's masterly criticism and mentioned my feelings about it. I received a card back, a printed form signed by Wilson that said Mr. Wilson does not do this and does not do that, leaving me wondering what he actually did do. Later, reading his memoirs of the twenties and thirties, I realize he kept pretty busy, getting married three times (I think it was three), and of course writing many books.

The letter sent to Roy Campbell was to the effect that now he was getting older he wouldn't be able to continue all the adventurous things he'd done in the past. Curt and I got a letter back listing everything he'd accomplished in the past year. It was truly incredible. I guess we'd touched some kind of nerve in Campbell's ego.

I can't remember what I said to Birney, but he too replied, inviting both Curt and me for lunch at U.B.C. where he was teaching. Of course we went, and were rather tongue-tied facing Birney's tremendous vitality and a flow of energy strong enough to gag Mount St. Helene's.

Both of us knew his poems well. But it was "Bushed," "Vancouver Lights," and "David" that made the most impression on me. "David" has received and merited a great deal of attention since. A few years ago I dramatized it into a half-hour radio play. And I believe Dorothy Livesay in her criticism as much as accused Birney of pushing his friend off that mountain. (The implication was very annoying to him.) The other two poems mentioned—well, I actually felt a bit reverent about them, sometimes repeating several lines to myself from "Vancouver Lights": can even remember the last part now without looking it up: "O stranger /Plutonian, beast in the crouching night/there was light." But I'd better look it up anyway. Okay, add "descendant" and make it "stretching night." Well, I was close.

Birney was always careful and solicitous about the welfare and encouragement of his students. (This attitude contrasted somewhat with my own feelings when I was writer-in-rez at various halls of learning. I thought few of the students really wanted criticism: all wanted to be called geniuses!) But this solicitude of Birney's was an active concern of his, a thing he practised.

One occasion sticks in my mind. I was in Vancouver, sleeping at a friend's apartment while the friend was off somewhere skiing. And in the morning heard a steady, persistent knocking at the door. It was Earle, and he wanted me to go with him down the street to his student's apartment. It seems this student in his creative writing class, a foreign exchange student at U.B.C., had not shown up that morning. And from various things she had told him about her husband, Earle thought he might be keeping her prisoner at their apartment, not allowing her to escape him on that bright autumn day.

I wasn't sure why my own presence was necessary in this possibly harmless domestic dispute, but Earle seemed to think so. Anyway, I was rushed into clothes and off we went—"just down the street."

A few minutes later, Birney knocked on their apartment door several times. No answer. Then we called on the superintendent, Earle explaining that he felt responsible for this student of his. She was a foreigner, and very young; there was a fatherly, avuncular, and trustworthy note in Birney's voice as he spoke. And I'm sure the super, facing this imposing professor of English, felt something close to awe, was almost flattered that his help was being sought.

The superintendent unlocked the apartment door with his master key. It was chainlocked from the inside. Birney talked through the narrow opening, calling softly to his student inside. Both she and her husband emerged. The girl, very tall, was wearing a housecoat. She and Birney talked in low tones, while I stood with her husband off to one side.

The husband was quite large and husky, wearing those white pyjamas jujitsu practitioners affect. He looked at me; I looked at him. He shrugged; I shrugged; we kept our faces expressionless. But I felt slightly embarrassed by this time, wondering what I'd gotten into. And Birney? He'd achieved his purpose, making sure his student was free to come and go to his classes.

What does all this have to do with Earle Birney's poetry? Well, I think it indicates strongly that he takes responsibility in both life and literature. Social responsibility, you could call it, and exemplified by his friendship and admiration for Leon Trotsky, the fugitive Russian revolutionary, before the last war. And by his personal sacrifices in that same war, from which he emerged with the rank of major.

The really wondrous thing about Birney—leaving his personality aside—is craft. And I know that sounds a bit mundane. But I mean CRAFT. He can take the most ordinary subject-thing and make it into a verse of nearly passionate interest. How? Through juxtapositions, word play, enjambments, images, and endings that circle back to something said at the beginning, and thereby often make the whole poem meaningful. But that attempt to analyze his methods says very little, because, in the end, I don't know how he does it.

"Still Life Near Bangalore" ends with a question. I'm

not sure what the answer to that question is and am not very interested anyway. From my view the real point to the poem is the completely fascinating "Still Life" itself. Sure, there are a lot more questions scattered through the poem; and I think the two-line question at the beginning has been added since I first read the poem several years ago. But what interests me are descriptions like: "Behind each slatey team an almost naked/human beast, bareheaded, breached with rags" describing a ploughman near Bangalore.

Other readers will, of course, find those questions of more interest than I do. To me, the poem is transport provided by Birney into Bangalore itself, the smells, the workmen, the talking women, the geography of an almost dream. And despite the exoticism of a far eastern country, mere description is often mundane: Birney makes it fascinating.

I should probably talk about only the poems included in this collection, at least that seems to me to be the general idea of writing an intro or preface for someone's book. But this is Birney's last book of poems. And he has been a very large presence in Canada, one that extends backward in time, and into the future, for I'm sure that his work will remain alive for a long time to come. My admiration for him also reaches out in many directions.

Acting as a critic (which I am certainly not), I believe his judgement of other people's work has been both relentless and kind. He went out of his way to help younger writers. I believe, in fact, that the creative writing course he established at U.B.C. was the first one in Canada. There was also that aforementioned responsibility to his students, and kindness to young writers. Earle has always been a man with passionate feelings for his own country, and at the same time his is a world view that encompasses all creation.

Does that seem to be saying a great deal—far too much? Am I being carried away on behalf of a friend? If it appears that way, then let me say also that he was both curmudgeonly and magnificent, close with money and wildly generous at the same time. A human being, that is. I have to explain that occasional past tense by mentioning that Birney suffered a serious illness four years ago, one that left him severely incapacitated.

Years ago, when I was struggling with machines in a Vancouver mattress factory, there were Birney poems that stiffened my spine. The previously mentioned "Vancouver Lights." The strange world of "Mappemounde" with medieval sailors sailing off the world's edge. The same poem's "That sea is hight Time/it hems hearts' landtrace"—over which, much later, I disagreed with his addition of "*all* hearts' landtrace," which served to touch every emotional base. I claimed the extra word wasn't needed. And "Bushed," that most Canadian of poems, in which the forest imprints itself on a man's brain as a country itself lives in human genes.

And now, in these "last makings," we traverse with Birney the long climb from childhood to young man and maturity and middle age to—quite old (although Earle was such a *bounding* man that decrepitude always seemed foreign to him). And travel by limey freighter to Grimsby, England in a sequence of poems that has the later Birney's scrambled-egg-words exemplifying his never-leave-em-alone work habits. And we linger over the sky and sea and mountain landscapes that spell British Columbia. As I look again at "Buoy off Juan de Fuca," I notice that I scribbled *wow!* on first reading it in my copy of the book. His love poems, and one about a girl's toes. Toes? Yes, toes. One

     so clean and succulent
     so tiny

> it's no toe at all
> but a spare nipple   ummmm

Well?

Three versions of "Ellesmereland" and another three of "Canada: Case History," the last trio also demonstrating something of the Birney method and movement from then to now.

There are many poems to Wailan:

> being twenty-seven she believes
> I can keep the sap alive
> even at seventy-two

> after three days
> the blossoms wreathe our floor

These Wailan poems are enchanting. They don't *seem to be* that way, they are. In some sense the whole book is Wailan, for Wailan, and of Wailan. Poems for her birthday, poems any day and all days. For her. The love of one being for another: and what else is there? – to paraphrase a certain blue-footed booby I once knew. Wailan on her 26th, 27th, 29th, and if you know Earle, you count them off until

> & never tell me when it's time
> that i'm to die
> or she's to leave me

but we do, dammit, we all do!

And this piece becomes my own farewell to Birney. I remember him best when he was at his best; striding the streets of Charlottetown when his picaresque novel, *Turvey*, was adapted into a musical play by Don Harron and Norman Campbell. You'd have thought he was twenty years younger than I instead of nearly twenty years older, the way he had to stop and encourage my

xvi

wife and me to keep going. (Our tongues were hanging out at the pace he set.) And one time, disagreeing over whether to take a cab or streetcar from Church Street to Spadina Avenue in Toronto: "For chrissake, Earle, I'll pay for the cab!" "That's not the point, Al. You're liable to want a beer later and need the money you spent on the cab."

Something quite magnificent about him at times; not phony, not the sort of guy who prepared "a face to meet the faces that you meet." A man joined to the texture of what he wrote about, Wailan, his country, the world.

Al Purdy
Ameliasburgh
November 1990

FYTTE THE FYRST

Deep goeth mood that driveth
out with seaflood to float
far from steading to stray
the wide whaleroad sailing
leaving lovers by hearth
from beership in meadhall bereft

1985

When I got whooping cough in Calgary the summer
                              I was seven
my Mum took me, a social outcast, to join Daddy
                              in a tent
tree-hidden near the darkgreen Bow that rimmed
                              Banff's village,
our only neighbours 2-month-cottage tourists, name of
                              Macklin.
I learned from Dad their kid was only five and
                              just a girl.
Dad was busy daytime up in town building us a house,
So Mum was stuck with cooking at the tent and
                              whooper me.

But the Macklins liked to ride the trails and climb,
and Mummy offered daytime care of Susan. She could
                              play with me
but I must keep arm's length away. Play what? I
                              mumbled.
Play catch, you've got a ball, or hide-and-seek,
                              play anything,
my Dad said, but mind you stay three feet away
                              from her
and don't go near the river. I sulked. I hadn't even
                              seen her yet.

Next day she came, a creature round and neat and
                              full of smiles.
She brought a skipping rope, a scooter. She called
                              me Ull.

4

My Daddy made a swing between two pines. I swung
                          her from behind
and never even touched the dimpled legs. Her pigtails
                          glittered
black as licorice in the sun. I was a skinny goof
with a carrot topknot. She never mocked my
                          noisy whoops.
I called her Sue and sailed her high and higher.

Out of Mother's sight one day, racing chipmunks
                          in the forest,
we stumbled on huge toadstools we pelted at the crows.
Then suddenly we came up on the Bow.

Silent we crept to its forbidden bank, looked down
                          to death,
into a twisting flow and seethe of dark unheeding waters
gliding so swift toward their falls. Wordless and separate
we lay, but linked in a spell of fear. Then fingers
                          touched.
We scrambled back, ran panting to the tent.

At August's end a wind with snowflakes
blew the first leaves yellow from the poplars
blew the last spasm from my throat
blew the Macklins far forever from the Birneys.

Yet no gale ever swept from memory my summer's
                          purest passion
for that armslength loving Sue
who never caught a whooping cough from me.

He swung me up on his shoulders
   Father-smell of his old Stetson
Now you can see

Seventy years under my skull
the right lobe feels/hears
that first town   first crowd
for a bush-ranch four-year-old
remembers all but words

Left brain finds these now

Ponoka Alta Fall Fair 1908 Main Street
   *Dom*dom in the face-forest *dom dom*
   something beats   partridge drumming?
   urgent *kye*yai shouts *dom*dom *dom*dom
Look Buster   Indians   a pow-wow
   I see only backs of fat ladies
   in blankets   they shuffle   seesaw
   *dom*dom droning *dom*dom*dom*dom
See son   inside the squaw-circle
   Yes! big manbirds hopping!
   Heads are feathers   on fire!
   Naked legs   moccasins in the dust
   *dom*dom black snakes whirling *dom*dom
   round their *dom*dom necks!
   I'm afraid! Snakes on the man-owls!
Blackfoot braves wear two braids
   Where is the partridge?
   Why do they hit it?

It's a tom-tom son   See   there's the drummer
And that's the Chief   with eagle feathers
   Hye-yai *kye*-yai   Are they mad at us?
No son   hungry   they're praying to their god
   What are they saying Daddie?
They say: send us deer meat   send elk
   Don't they like eggs either?
They're Blackfoot   They like to hunt their food
Ponoka is their word for Elk
They eat wild ducks too   and rabbits
but there's not enough of those now
   *Dom*dom *dom*dom *kye-yai-kye-yai-kye-yai*!
   I hate turnips   I want to hunt elk!
   *Dom*dom I want to hit the *tom*tom
No no you stay on my shoulder
It's like their church son   It's a deer-dance
   Can we do tomtom in our church Daddie?
Tom-tom is just for them Buster
Like the organ is for us
They're trying to bring deer back
so they won't have to be farmers
   *Dom*dom Why are we far-DOM!
   Drum stops

   The Chief is talking to us
   His face is big and stern
   He looks like God   Is he Eagle-God?
   I wish *he* were my grandfather
   He would take me hunting
   We would catch elk too
   Now he has a black hat in his hand
   The crowd is moving away
Daddie puts me down   reaches in his pocket
"The poor devils must be half-starved

When he brings the hat near you
put these quarters in from us."
    There are just a few dimes and nickels
    Don't they grow things to sell, Daddie?
Not much Buster   They've got swampy soil
even worse than ours

Early frost and snow that week
Daddie is hanging wallpaper in Edmonton
so we can buy winter clothes Mom says
and feed for the animals
    *Pom*pom *pow*wow bangclang bang
    I squat by kitchen stove *pow*wow
    I bang a broken pot *brong brong brong*
    Da-dee take me *hunt*ing *bang* brong
    Da-dee come back *soon* soon
    Hye-yai *kye*-yai *h*aiyaikaiyai
Child! Spare my hearing!
    *Dom*dom I am *Black*foot I am *Chief*
    I will bring back *deer*
O Buster there *are* no deer   not any more
Come and eat your porridge while it's warm
    *Dom*dom*brong*! We are *Black*foot
    We *don't like farming*.

1979

That nightfall, when Dad rode back with mail,
he read us from the *Calgary Herald* about the comet.

"The weather's cleared. Moon down. After chores
let's all walk up the turnip hill and look for Halley."
"I've bread in the oven," Mother said. "You two go on,
and tell me later."

Alone above the dead-black woods we stared
into the blazing sky.
Near us an owl who-whoed.
I clung to my father's leathery hand.
There could be bears below.
"That's it!" he pointed, helped me find the haze
in the glittering millions.
A smudge with a streaky tail.
"Will it get lots bigger, Daddie?"
"Maybe, Buster. But remember it now, the way it is.
It won't be back till the nineteen-eighties!"

"It'll be bigger then," I said hopefully.
"And Mom will come and we'll all see it together."
"I'll long be dead when it's here again, son,
but you might live to see it."

I pulled my hand away, betrayed somehow.
"No, no. We'll see it together."
I knew some old people died, and cats, but not my Dad!
Not any of us. "We'll see Halley again, won't we? Dad?

Again and again?" His big hand circled mine once more, but he didn't answer.

1986

PORT ALBERNI TO GRIMSBY
BY LIMEY FREIGHTER, 1934

I. Last Night in Harbour: Captain Bullthorp

Still red from thundering at the second mate,
young meek and milky Mr. Foote,
because a deck plank gave beneath a seaman's weight
scattering bagged potatoes to the scuppers,
the Captain stuffs the momentary spoils of land
into his tough old belly: fresh eggs and liver,
watermelon, a touch of whisky from his private
cache, into a sugar-heavy tea. Freddy the steward
scuttles out; the Captain in His messroom always
dines alone, square in the middle of his table,
square beneath his bridge. His portholes now
are blocked high with lumber chained to the fore-deck,
a sprawling prisoner any storm might free.
The Captain chews his meat in silence
and the deepening night.

II. Alberni "Canal": Departure

These firs already breathed when old
Pedro Alberni, Captain and Don
sailed into Nootka Sound to hold
with a hundred troops in his galleon
this pounding coast from Englishmen—
and quickly luffed away again
leaving only his stranger's name
to serve his channel and his fame

No man-grubbed ditch is this lank
lance the ocean thrusts unbending
deep into the scaly flank
of George Vancouver's Island: rending
glaciers alone have trenched
this giant gorge, and nothing less
than tilting continents have drenched
and drowned its floor in quietness
a hundred fathoms down   Today

the inlet's fretted crests are lost
in white obliteration, frost
of hillcloud sliding down to lay
a numb annihilation straight
along the mountain's bony knees
Above that line the gauzy trees
dissolve like ghosts caught out too late

III.   ka pass age alaska passage ALASKA PASSAGE *alaska passage alas*

our ship seems reefed
and only the land comes swimming past alaska pass

the f_{irs}tthro_{ugh}   g_re e n   ^cr_{es}c_en   t_ot_he
_tr_{am}p_do_wn_wthe^fo_g i n   D_O   ^fO_R
               _ar_{ds}   E/

SHO _re'S p^le_D c_OM_mo^t_ioⁿ _of _br_is^tl^e^d
                                   R_O C K_S

_an^d b l a n c h i n g   d r i f
                                         t

u^P_fr_om a sp^e^w   ^sp_l& B_a   L_og_ch^ut^e^w^s
               _of   _in_te_rR K A   A^rr_o
                      _s

(one mark of few that men have scribbled
on this lucky palimpsest of ranges)

at times a shake-built shack exchanges
passive stares with Come & Gone
or eyeless waits with stoven side
^{to} slide _{its} bones _{in} a
                       g^r e e n t i d e

age alaska passage alaska passage alaska passage alas-ka
pass

IV. *Lifeboat* (first version)

Sudden squawk from the loading-mast peak
gets drowned in a crash of metal on deck
between us and a lifeboat's launching davits
We deckhands gawk at a scramble of tackle
ropes hawsers writhing still   Missed
our heads by inches   Appearing at once
from nowhere Bert the bosun shoots a flame
of words aloft at a boy-sized Malay
who is gesturing dumbly with an empty hook
the tackle was too heavy for him   We seamen
stand half in spell at Bert's oration
but my scalp tingles and I breathe my thanks
to whatever sea god steered this ton of death
away from our innocent necks   The bosun of course
ignores us but fires a parting shot up the mast

    you useless son of a poxed cunt it's lucky
    for you you missed the fuckin davits you . . .

IV. *Davits* (second version)

A sudden cry from the foremast top
drowns in the crash of metal on the deck
beside us. We gawk wordless at a scramble
of tackle, rope and hawsers writhing still.
It had all missed by a foot a lifeboat's davits
on one side and our heads on the other.
At once the First Mate has materialized
from nowhere and is shooting flames up
at a boy-sized Malay who is gesturing dumbly,
with an empty hook, the tackle was too heavy
for him. I half-listen to the Mate in appreciation
but my scalp still tingles. I breathe thanks
to whatever gods had steered this ton of death
from our innocent necks. The mate ignores us
but wings a parting shot up the mast:

> Lucky for you you useless son of a poxed cunt
> you didn't hit those davits.

V. Barkley Sound

Down the marching fjord our freighter
slides god-sped by gullish Pater-
noster past Indians motionless
and smudged in fishing-tubs, past mess
of snaggled log and tombstone stump
where axe and greed and fire have spread
the forest's macaronic dead
past high-rigged sparpole, sawdust dump
past one swart tugboat harbour-bound
and into heaving Barkley Sound

Its waters lie as wide and lonely
as when young Barkley risked his only
schooner and a schoolgirl bride
to tack ashore by unscaled tide
with beads and bullets from Stoke and Clyde
and reap the rare sea-otter's hide

The last point fades; we lie again
above our hundred-million-year-old home
Across an Asia-reach of wave the winds
compute their ceaseless algebra of foam.

VI. Buoy off Juan de Fuca

Vulnerable and determined as a marsupial's fetus
our ship has crawled new-hatched from Port Alberni
onto the fog-wrapped edge of the Pacific's belly.
In the swells the *Filly* heaves her ten thousand tons
of wheat and lumber and clinging sailors past
this last writhing mouth of British Columbia.
The funnel's horn breathes pneumonic warnings
of invisible shoals, unheard ships. Suddenly
we are struggling to veer away from a presence,
an iron skeleton no bigger than my own, rising
on foam-hidden feet, poising at the waters' will.
It blinks a bloodshot eye, sinks with a human moan.
I cling, a green deckhand, to the nearest stanchion.
Our wireless taps out messages to nothing. Alien
and desolate, I flinch from the yowls of this monster,
ambiguous friend, ghoul that winks distraught
and howls to be free, to sink at last with us
to darkness and silence. A chained leper it serves
only by howling us off. How many tugs, log rafts,
freighters has its master, the reef, devoured before us?
Am I the only one chained to this deck by my fear?
It is a thing out of my own Unconscious.
It is a warning buoy . . . . The *Filly* passes.

1934/1985

VII. *Flying Fish off Salvador*

From the basalt waves we flake
bronzed and blue as dragonflies,
flash into the alien air
skip and flutter at the sky
almost soar   but stall and fall
flicker back into our mirror
Not from play or zest in flight
but in gauzy fishy terror
we the sea's most desperate charges
beat against the bars of light
Below our finger fuselage
invisible the Devil slides
huge behind our tautened wingbooms
rolls our round eternal Wrath
Tuna twines   or Porpoise loops
no take-off that will set us loose
to follow in the swallow's path
no wingspread yet beyond the gauge
of the Devil's callipers.

Suddenly   dancing ahead of our bow
is a flashing procession of beings.
They jolly our lumbering freighter
and beautifully cleanly rocketing
out and curving in to the curving waves.
Black wedges gleam from their bluegrey backs
and all are supple and silent and swift
as sharks.

But these creatures would seem to be treating us
merely as guests at their ballet.
Humans not only in length but in vanity
they divert themselves by performing
to deckhands . . . . Dolphins?
"Nah," says the old salt from Grimsby, "poepuss.
Dawfins is in t'Atlantic. Poepuss . . . pigfish
some call 'em. They chasin smallfry, squid mebbe,
wot the ship stirs up." The bosun chips in:
"Not worth the catchin' either, them piggies,
too oily to eat." (The sun slides behind a cloud.
The dancers vanish without waiting for encores.)
Ping goes the ship's bell, ping ping.
"Now git movin', you lubbers. Git this deck swabbed."

Housman   Keats   & even Rimbaud
sniffed only joy from all those flambeaux
blazing from their chestnut trees
& cherry blossoms in the breeze

no ragweed grew on a Shelley green
romantic veins lack histamine

Hampstead Heath 1935

DECREE ABSOLUTE (FOR ESTHER)

we remember strangely the first hurts from love
the young are pierced through by their passions

you must not grow ancient   poor dear
but quickly old enough to forget
this last aggression

it will be enough to carry
to our separate deaths
the memory of the first time
i stung you to tears

twenty-five and loving and we at last together
while beyond the window of our train
all Kent was singing with appleblossoms
shaken by the bees

Canterbury 1935 – Toronto 1975

THAT NIGHT

that night you said would have this worth
until our ribs were hoops of earth
that when an august moon swims high
whatever miles apart we lie
we'll match the same grey seashelf sliding
down to the fountaining waves & hiding
our slyer selves from prying relatives
clocks & creeds & their correlatives

i said we would remember too
that stone we watched the tide suck through
till it turned to a seal in the moon

but memory is time's buffoon
& i this night can scarce recall
your glimmering body weasel small
& you will never quite recover
this long insatiate surging lover

sleep that coils us in our shells
toils different dreams from jangled bells

tonight you lie an ocean away
a bomber's moon pales in my day
& words can help us now as much
to reattain that night as crutch
would aid us walk our separate ways
past all the moons in the milky ways.

England 1943

I. *Leaping to Mexico 1956*

Nimble as springboks to soar in one hop
from Vancouver's midnight and chill rain
to radiance in mysterious Mexico.
How liberating to clear two sets of customs
excise immigration vaccination non-immigration
plant control and loyalty oaths to God and senators
with bullying jowls in Washington, D.C.

Once in the air, of course, the State of Washington
became charming embroidery
unrolling anagrams of village lights,
Boise, Idaho—a little grid of rubies
and diamonds, concealing republicans,
the right-wing democrats in Denver just
a star cluster
Roadlights faded out among non-voters.

Clouds came and there was only
our prop plane, its stubby carrot halo-tipped
and every rivet frosted,
solid above the emptiness
we never quite forgot in those days

Then the first touch of the hidden
Godfinger spreading a chalky quadrant
on the slate of night
hardening a blur into ranges

quickly now igniting air and earth
to sooty flame
The omnipotent Sun broke clouds
to cloudlets which the endless belt of air
drew towards us, under, and away

Clear then but safely far below
a small society floated on petrol
laid out its games with dominoes and checkers,
doll palaces of oil on the great Texan table
where roads from everywhere twisted aside
we crossed the Rio Grande

into a morning land of pumice
spored with sagebrush, or was it mesquite?
(I'd never seen mesquite)
Cacti, perhaps, the specks on grey hairs of canyons
Where were the people?
A land of melted chocolate

Cumulus darkened overwhelmed
We mounted into mastering light
blazing its own Antarctica
bergs pack-ice with cracks that narrowed down
deliriously to nothing

A half-hour and we sank again
into the furrows of a giant's plough
But these mountains had colour
in their desiccation, surrounded a valley
lakes avenues houses—
Popocatepetl winked a white eye once
and slid behind his curtain

Light as fleas we landed in the high air
over heaven's hedge
jumped the fat waist of a continent
spun heady through the first elegant
airport I'd ever seen and past
officials with smiles and manners

Buenos días, Mexico
can we be neighbours at last?

COMMONWEALTH ARTS FESTIVAL WEEK, 1965, CARDIFF, A COLLAGE (AS COVERED BY THE WELSH PRESS)

MACK THE KNIFE IS PICK OF FIELDS
Greatest race starts from the Welsh College
General William Westmoreland said and
one of the unsolved mysteries of the war is
the so-called Poetry Festival in Cardiff
KNIFE THE PACK AND FICK THE REELS
a British Captain disappeared from Saigon
wanted by the Commonwealth Arts Festival
seven months ago with two sisters
he agrees to lift ban on phosgene in Vietnam
PAT THE PICT IS WIFE OF WALES
Archdruid interrupts Commonwealth Poets
some censorship is better than amateur basketball
but said he preferred a free society
without art or Anita Ekberg
of course has full authority from Washington
to use ordinary tear gas but
one of the sisters aged sixteen
a smash hit at the Berlin Ystrad Mynach
has refused to say anything about the last two months
PICK THE MUCH IS BARTERED BRIDE
Glam-Mon Motors Proudly Presents
The Immaculate Con
but not the lethal kind
for so-called artists trying to tear down society
MICK THE MACK IS FIELD OF PICTS
Immaculate Consul 1965
never rallied never raced

The U.S. Military Commander
and the Topless Dancer have now
returned to Saigon and the mystery singers
while the Exhibition of Christian Art
has had to move
from the so-called Poetry Festival in Cardiff
but Welsh theatre proudly presents
"Lovely Gift of the Gab"
as Archdruid interrupts Commonwealth Poets
a pantomime of revels from old Jamaica
NICK THE EX AND PUCK THE FEELS
Reg-begs you are, reg-begs,
an Australian journalist shouted
mingled with the rhythms of Africa
Topless dance against their will
which will certainly appeal to some
but a so-called Vietnam pig was hired
never rallied never raced
from a private zoo in Cardiff
seven months ago with two sisters
never sullied never raped
a huge spotted creature
has the right to appeal of course
from the Asian jungles
but the Archdruid demanded equal time
without art or Anita Ekberg
to recite battle songs in Welsh
while an Australian journalist read his verse
POETS LET PIG LOOSE IN WELSH NATIONAL MUSEUM
a smash hit at the Ystrad Mynach
MUCK THE NUCK IS PICK OF FIELDS
Black poets allege hotel discrimination
but not the nausea-provoking riot kind

from the Asian jungles
wanted by the Commonwealth Poets
someone who can work a one-handed bellows
for the Immaculate Consul at the Odeon . . .
Foreign Poets Riot—involve local art school . . .
Archdruid Repudiates Poets . . .
MACK THE KNIFE STILL PICK OF FIELD

THREE FOR ALISON

1. *i think you are a whole city*

& yesterday when i first
touched
you i started moving
thru one of your suburbs
where all the gardens are fresh
with faces of you
flowering up

some girls are only houses
maybe a strip
development
woman you are
miles of boulevards   with supple
trees unpruned & full of winding
honesties

so give me   give me
time   i want   i want
to know all your squares &
cloverleafs   ime steering now
by a constellation winking over
this night's rim from some great
beachside of you with highrisers & a spotlit
beaux arts

i can hear your beating centre will i
will i make it   are there maps of
you i keep circling   imagining parks
fountains arcades all your stores

back in my single bed
i wander
your stranger   dreaming
i am your citizen

The Beaches, Toronto 1965

2. *there are delicacies*

there are delicacies in you
    like the hearts of watches
there are wheels that turn
    on the tips of rubies
& tiny intricate locks

i need your help
    to contrive keys
there is so little time
    even for the finest
            watches

Scarborough 1966

3. *i should have begun with your toes*

with maybe just the little one
so clean & succulent
so tiny
it's no toe at all
but a spare nipple   ummmm

now the big one
big? the nail on it so weeny
& silvery
it's more like a stamp-hinge
to hold down some rarity
a pink imperforate
engraved in *taille douce*

& you've got ten
all in mint condition

& now let's forget
philately
& up the golden stairs!

Waterloo, Ont., September 1967

Sep. 5
2 p.m. Decide to cross from south to west Australia by
train. Adelaide friends grip my hand in silent parting.
Ticket office says only single compartments left
    kawzefflahturz.
Because of flatterers? floaters? no? eh?
    Kawzeffflaw season in Wessen Stryleya.
O Flower Tours! Of course! Spring is sprung and Perth
is take-off point for desert wildflowers. I'll learn this lan-
guage yet! . . .
The Aussies bigger than the seats and all seats filled. Is
that what's flattened half the wheels already? A sweaty
worm I go through the palsied coaches, looking for my
single compartment.
    Eyent nen (says the surly conductor)
But here's my ticket. It says sing—
    You gotta chynge trynes fust. Chynge et Pert Peery.
But my tick—
    Gotta chynge guyjiz fust.
Guyjiz? O gauges! I understand. How long to Port Pirie?
    *Six ahs, mite. Troy the cleb car. Git a beeah enny-
wye.*
In the club car the beer's all drunk, but the barmen pro-
mise a fresh supply at next stop. I settle on somebody's
chair-arm. It's like Vancouver's Cordova Street at clo-
sing time.

8:20 p.m. Across a windy platform I carry my bags to a
wider train and a compartment at last. The coach is a
cave with just enough light to read the notice at the

door: NO POWER IN COMPARTMENTS AFTER 8 p.m. . . .
Before I can back out, the train has lurched away with
me. Powerless to read, drink, eat, or leave. Suddenly it's
cold. Hunched under my one blanket I try by the win-
dow to write in the half-light but the train keeps
throwing me like a clinched bronco. Maybe I could get a
cup of tea? My buzzer, an hour later, produces a train-
man. He has only a hot-water bottle to offer. Full. And
quite cold. I take a pill.

Sep.6
7:00 a.m. Head tight and solid as cabbage. Outside the
window a monochrome flat-brushed landscape. Occasion-
al saltbush speckling an occasional rock. Every 5 miles
a crow. Vegetable survivors in the flatness dwindle to
nothing. And nothing circles these decrepit stations we
don't even pause for . . . Then we need water, but all
doors and windows are locked while we take it on.

12:00 noon. Space is the enemy we are guarded from, as
we wait to be fortified with strong beer and stronger
mutton. Meanwhile the limestone takes over from the
dolomite, and even the saltbush quits. My map says my
train is now launched on a 300-mile straightaway. But it
lurches worse than ever, on a bender without a bend,
wubbling and lullupping along like a Giant Pram.
   Saryles werp fruh meat someone volunteers across
the aisle. I get it the third time: It's so hot out there it
warps the rails! (And like the Gobi, just as cold at
night.) At last I manage my own warp, around a matron
wide as a Rubens, and close-haul to avoid males even
bigger, and into half a seat beside her. She has been ex-
changing waves and toots with sister ships in the table's

other two seats. One of these, as we wait for our fried
sheep, turns conversationally to me:

    Air yew anna terr?

Or a tare? O, *tour*! Why yes, but how could you know?!
(Did she see my pix in the Sydney papers?) Before she
can answer one of the others is flooring me with another
question:

    Yew nemma wunna nemma tew?

Number one what? Canada's best or secondbest? I'm
flattered but before I've betrayed my narcissism my Ru-
bens explains. They had assumed I was, like them, on
one of the two Flower Tours this train was ferrying.
Half are to go south from Perth, half north.

No, I say fatuously, I'm touring for poesie not posies.
But the three of them stare at me with disappointed and
suspicious eyes straight from a Sidney Nolan painting.

I mean we're all botany buffs anyway, I say. I am res-
cued by the landscape—turning from blankness suddenly
to trees, eucalyptus reddening in the sunset. We rattle off
the Nullarbor onto a gold reef.

    Real beaut they all agree about the sunset. *Chynge
trines* says the conductor.

Kalgoorlie, says my guide book, in 1893 the world's rich-
est square mile. We all hump bags again across another
gyge. The new train's locked.

    Kembeck enna hower, says trainman over his shoul-
der, *toime ta see Kalgoorlie. Lift a few.*

The gold fever withered it. A ghost town for an Aussie
Pierre Berton. And they've run out of beer.

Back at the train, it's open now, my bags are in a com-
partment for two, and an ancient Tasmanian chain-
smoker has staked out the lower berth. We both produce

single tickets for the conductor. He reads them and smiles jovially.

Yeh-yeh. Singles oright but eyent now singles innis tryne.

sleep comes   and goes   the night passes somehow

Sep.7
With dawn there is a five-house galvo "town" with balding grass, every roof every fence is dull tin or rusting iron, only the names make melodies:
Bullabulling   Woolgangie   Kellerberrin, the aboriginal poetry of place outlives its poets

And now strange as a science fiction cover
a real stream with ducks under flowering wattles
and more Nolan women waving mechanically from porches
I ask what river. *Ivan*, my Tasman mutters.
The Russians were here? I check my map. *Avon* of course.
Between the villages now the wildflowers take over:
Great bushes Reckitt's blue, plains solid yellow,
hills sheeted white or polka-dotted
Through it all our alien train slides
its human enzymes busy breaking down
their muttonfat with beer

Just before Perth a drove of sheep
with big green splotches crop
beside a row of nine bright shithouses
and no habitations—I'm on a different planet
One of my Rubens ladies says now to the other
    Thaze pertsa newsuf wiles loy keer
and the other agrees:
    Ng-yay-yaze, I orris sighs a olewells a sime reely

Tazmineya Viktoeya . . .
Yazen yew tike New Sealints   chiss loike Swisalin
some people wunta gown runnabaht Yewrup
wennay cudavvit ollit owm . . .
Ngyay-yaze, owmz best, wnya thenka battit

Noon   and the Swan River   detergent foam
Perth   the Indian Ocean   Freedom!

Perth, Australia 1968/1985

The painter quiets all but his busy brush.
The writer is obsessed to ask: what next?

My train creeps blindly through this canvas
towards old Bangalore. Nearest my window,
right, an oxcart moves (or stops?)
on a pinched black road where jacarandas
leave magenta bruises, and a pair of women
stand face to shadowed face beneath tiered baskets.
They are compositions of sky-blue shawls
and sable braids aslant down chalky saris.
Merchant's wives, I'd guess, with time to gossip.
Left, their road elbows, vanishes with palms.

Beyond the oxcart the emerald paddyfields
submit to yoked brute buffalo.
Indifferent geometrists they draw in ochre mud
their sinuous counter-patterns.
Behind each slatey team an almost naked
human beast, bareheaded, breached with rags,
is ploughing (with a stick, is it?, clutched
in raddled hands) while a companion guides
their Shivas by a rope. It threads the sacred
nostrils. They steer around the corpse-like
sleeping cows and boulders huge as bones
of long-drowned mastodons.

The background, between bamboo strokes
and breadfruit blobs, is giving hints
of lizard-tawny thatch (the village

of those still, still-talking matrons?)
Near a splash of wall where a *flamboya* burns
dim figures walk with trays, perhaps of frangipani
for an unseen temple. Or of sandalwood?
(My window cannot smell.)

But what kind of cloud on that horizon
is swelling silently from jungle into sky?
And what will happen here beside me
as round the bend to Bangalore
comes sudden mounting filling the road
a ten-ton oil truck? It is surely
roaring, blaring, screeching out its warnings?
(My window cannot hear.)

In that second when they slid forever from my ken
did those women leap away? that cloud subside?
Or towered to fill their sky with fire so bright
no painter's brush no writer's thought
will ever stay to catch it?

India 1972

ROT BELOW ADAM'S PEAK (SRI LANKA)*

Coming down on the train from Kandy
under curvy clouds and whorls
beyond whorls of mountains
i stare at the jungle wall

Sometimes black rock startles
skulls of forgotten volcanoes
that set Sir Island ablaze
But the forest resumes
greenness denser than oceans
concealing even its worst
terrors

which are not the leopard
shrinking his golden flanks
from human sighting
the small crocodile sliding away
the sloth-bear testy in orchids

The horror lies
where my friend walked
peering through stink
at his two graduate students
in the bough-darkened stream
awash and roped together

Their bloated faces   demon-eyed
stalked with him back
stripped him wordless
before his beautiful living children

Shot stabbed clubbed for the jackals
by the soldiers their older brothers
a thousand idealists lie early to rot
behind all this verdure

Give tongue to these spectres
and you will join them

For a space my train runs above the valley
and I glimpse the Sacred Peak
where Adam, Buddha, Mohammed, someOne, nobody
left a footprint in lava

Descending our engine slows
around another swart outcrop
Two brown monkeys caught playing
on the rock-face freeze   stare   skip
arc   vanish through the treewall
into that fourth dimension
we forever lost

*1972—shortly after unsuccessful rebellion against the
dictatorship of Mrs. Bandaranaike by high-school stu-
dents, who were machine-gunned in the woods while
bound and helpless.

cat kills mouse
or is it mouse
kills cat?

Psst! every mouse
cat
kills
cat will
eat
and mouse
meat
will
slow
cat's
will
to kill
till
starved cat
lies still

Ergo mouse
kills cat.

1973

a sound has roused me   a gull screeching?
no   it's night still   i slip from our hostel bed
to the balcony   the Big Dog is leashed
to the bright nail of Sirius in a silence
almost absolute   i hear only a dying cough
from the lone watchman below in the camel-yard
and in a smudge of palms the Saharan winds
scratching like crabs   i turn back to bed

but suddenly again that cry
a woman's voice   not near   not far   urgent
from that maze of workmen's tents by the dam?
peril or nightmare? a passion sped that scream!
i think fear . . . but of what?   rape?   murder?

i have no phone   no Arabic   only male guilt
beyond my railing now the dawn blurs
over Elephant Island, those rocks the Nile gnawed
to a funeral boat immense enough to ferry
fifty centuries of Nefertitis off to Nowhere
brief bark of a dog   Canubis   half-wild now
by the edges of tombs, the guide said
guarding still   or howling a mate?
the human call is not repeated

behind i hear my dearest waking murmurous
from a dream of bawdry (with me, she says)
her artless laughter sets me on fire

as naked in the sheets we launch once more
with wanton cries the fragile vessel
of our own brief day

Egypt 1974

Now was the season
summer so high and still
the birds in the circling woods
held all the tale

Past deserted nests I rose
through a world of web with swede-saw
severing
dropping
the black treebones
for the consummation of winter fire
O through the brace and embrace
of a hundred living arms I swung
gathering delight in my own ease
muscle and breath at a play of skill

I was climbing the tall beech
to prune dead limbs
that overhung the summer home
before some gale might hurl
a snag into glass

Each grasp tugged at the old zest
for a climb:
the rock-fort a year back
in Sri Lanka
and before in my sixties
up the yellow spines of Australia's Olgas . . .
at fifty-eight in the cloudy Andes on the ribs
of Huayna Picchu at thirty

inching down English chalk on Lulworth cliffs
. . . twenty-one and over the icy necks
of the Garibaldis and before that
the cliffs of my teens . . . Temple . . .
Edith . . . all the climbings
made in joy of the sport
and never with hurt to me or to others

as now to the topmost vault
of the beechtree's leaves I rose
to the flooding memories
of childhood
perched in my first treehouse
safe in its green womb

Where brittle branches had threatened
a tunnel of light
shone up to me now
as i sat in the secrets of leaf
and smiled on the innocent roof
that hid my love preparing our noon-day meal

Shining ahead was the fortnight
given us here alone by our friends
to swim with the small fish in their pond
read and doze in the sun
hide in the sumac to watch
the little fox by their den
or to work with hands on wood
and heart on words
rhythms already shaping themselves
in the piney air
this first of the mornings

So I threw the last snag down
and the locked saw after
turning and shifting my grips
to descend to Wailan
when something   my Hubris
some Fury of insect wing and sting
drove its whining hate at my eye
One hand unloosed
convulsive to shield
and I slipped
forever from treetops

Caught in a yielding chair of air
I grasped and grasped
at a speeding reel
of branches half-seized
and wrenched away
by the mastering will
of the earth
The next bough surely—
my hard mother
crushed me limp in her stone embrace
stretched me still
with the other limbs
laid my cloven hip and thigh
with those I had cleft

And that was a world
and two summers ago
yet still in the night I reach
for holds eluding my clutch
till the moment comes
when the Furies
relent

I catch and cling
swoop
alight on friendly ground

and run again on two good feet
over the grass of dream

Toronto 1977

PRAYER

our father who art
the positive particle's
particle
forgive us not
our daily increase
as we forgive not the other species

lead us not into further complexity
but deliver us
from ourselves

for thy atom will re-form
and thy pulsing be somewhere done
in life as in death

for whatever is ever
with or without
us

Eire, May 1977

49

there's a great snow-bank-job
in the university's MS collection
kept below melting
all the pleas boasts i love yous
snaps clips pix posters IOUs
sincerelys xxxes
everything insoluble in air
the world blew up around me

but the best friends
there was seldom need to write
and relatives had nothing to say

whatever was edible
dissolved long ago on the ghostly tongues
of perplexed parents
and frustrated teachers

a few books
but they are lies lacking nutrition
written by others
i once was

only my true love knows
what morsels are left
and she will not use them
to feed your image

University of Stirling, July 1977

TRAWNA TUH BELVUL BY KNAYJIN PSIFIK

(for Ron & Lorna Everson)

Tickets!   Wear yuh goan?   Tickets!   Oshwa? Upta en
upta *en   faren.*   Tickets tickets!
Wear you goan Oshwa?   Oh *Otwa* right dare first coach
Wear yuh goan?   Trennon?   Upta en
Belleville?   Upta en en en yeah Hurry tup . . . .
Awwwwww *bord*! . . . Aw bord . . . . Bore . . . . *Bord!*

Uhmn hunhun Uhmn Ay du dun   *day* duh dun
day duh duh *day* duh duh
WACKITY duh duh WACKITY CLAG CLANG duh duh
WANGDITTY KLONG
duh DUB de dub deDUB de dub de DRUB de DRUB
de WANGITY WACKLEDEE GELACK GELACK
DUB de dub de DUB de dub de didee
Dub de Didee   Dub de Didee de didee de dee
past the Guild and blast the mills
and whatta lotta whatta lotta lotta autos lotta autos
o good grayshun land of goshen autos waitin
autos banded by the station for the GO train
on we rush   skirting the bluffs   swirling the roughs
starling the puffs   the smelling the luffs
the luff the lufflee flowers the weeds the flowers
the weeds in the ditch   always a ditch
tall with weeds and full of shitch
that fits a ditch but not the flowers
bowers in the whitch?   towers of kitsch   flowers for rich
KLANITY BANG CANG   Can cans in the ditch

no plans for the ditch
log in the ditch   dog by the ditch
dog after bitch   rogue after tits   poles with the ditch
always the poles poles and poles and slow int-oo Whit-
WAKKITY KLANG into what? into Whit into WHIT BEEEEE
Whitby!   Ay duh dah duh   fhnn nmmm
Anyone fer Whitby? Out *this* door
CLANGITY WHAM BONK   clumpity bong . . . .
Awwww BORD . . . . *Bord!*

Uhmn Uhmn Ay dahdun   DAY duh dun day   DAY duh
de died de dee beside the sea beside the LAKE
beside the Lake   beside the see teeheee
beside the lakesea   the sealake   and theres a ship
& whats after Whit? apart from a ditch? a scarp on a slake
WALKITY KANG DE DIEDEEAdee   de wen de leevy
O when you leave a   little station and
goo cheevin hoo the nation   wen you leaf a leetle patience
and go chuggin thru the marmacans so buggin to
the marmaland go joggin thru the marmalade the BOOOOOO
the bish the bird the bush the bard the bosh
the birch the barm the farm alarm the harm
the barn the barmy farmlands   the squirmy wormlands
where there arent so many farmers   not a farmhand not a—
dots of oil tanks lots of gravel   pots of houses all alike

theres a factory making tractories   baking trucks and
faking cars and tracks and lime and making time
may king sweat shirts may king time and grime and dimes
making making making hay
nnnwrooooo . . . . oooooo oo de DEB de didy
DUB de did Dud de OSHee dub de OSHAWA! Oshwaaa
Ay de fnnm KLANG ITY bumMM   step down . . .
Boy up   Mombaby up

. . . . Awla*bord!* . . . . KLANGITY . . . . Ay de fnnnm de diddle
de drub de drub de WAMGOTY WACKITY
Dob de doe de dub de boe de Boe de BOWMANVILLE
Bowmanville Bowmanville that was Bowmanville
that was Bow-Diddety *dee* ditty *ded* daddy de
KRANG GRANDKIXIG day klasses   baby dozes   boy doesnt
de kassay de hiss-hissy de kaskastle
bluecattle NEW CASTLE newcastle   WAKKITY CLANG

Ontario, July 1977

Liquid steel the harbour stirs
is mercury under the Wind
   the Wind down Labrador from Baffin
   twisting always east
   in the topspin of our whirling world

bobbing the naked masts
of *Inacio Cunha* (Oporto 1970)
of *Elisabeth* (Fernando Po)
driven in from the Banks
a long roadstead of ships
and their crewmen jostling
   as the Basques were harried
   the *Guipuscoans*
   blown to these hard coves
   before Caboto   before Colombo
leaving their word for cod
on the lips of the Beothuk
and on Mercator's chart
terra de baccalos

Stripped of sail still they jump
the old hulks prance to the air's call
weave their sterns in a sarabande
of Maltese crosses
between Amerigo's oldest town
and the ocean's older maw

   This is the air a few days back
   that whistled around Pt. Barrow

came over the Beaufort
howling across the Boothia
and over Hudson's Bay as once
it howled over Hudson dead
over Franklin dying
and before them the first pre-Dorsets
lasting it out in snowpits

Around the latest concrete towers
the storm blusters
and into the rocky throat
    the Labrador icecap drilled
    a few millennia back
    from the last peninsula out to the bed
    of that lost Champlain Sea

The gale mouths abrasion
thickens the dusk with scour
from the bloodred cliffs
licks dirt from the sprawling finger-pier
gnaws at the rust on the playground cannon
that once barked pirates away
•
This wind that turns the Polar Cap
    elbowed the Vikings south to Vinland
    with crystals of ice bloodied their beards
    shouted Giovanni Caboto down from Belle Isle
    shoved Fagundes around Cap de Raz
    and turned John Rut back home to England

Tonight it shreds green paint
from the jogging prow of another *Pinto*
rubbing through to the rib-patterns
that trail back to Polo's Venice

Over Signal Hill it climbs unflagged
unflagging   its messages only moans
through scrawny wires and the tatters of moss
unhooked and swirling over the cliffs
Spume rides through the dark
from the upcoast waves
spatters the Tower's memorial plaque
    that remembers newcomers
    blundering in from Bristol
    a mere five centuries back
    No epitaph for the bears
    or the Beothuks

an absence that never gives pause
to the illiterate Wind on the Hill
gouging a little deeper
the seaward scores of the ghost glacier
    vanished long before the Cabotos
    before Leif and Torvald
    and Bjarni killer of Skralings
    our glacier gone but not forgotten
    the Old One planning return
    But not as old as the western Wind
    that girdled whatever was north
    before even the oceans cooled
    and the plates of the world's hide drifted

In its own caprice the twining Wind
may puff this year safely to haven
all the boats bloody with skins of the doomed seal
or leave the clubbers to drift in fog
and be clubbed by the ice

This air
    that throbbed for Marconi

bending to the first leap of speech over ocean
rides deaf to the east as ever
wordless beats against Europe
   as it beat back to their deaths
   who knows how many venturing Phoenicians
   what monks in a tub from Eire
   This is the passionless Gyre
   that held Cartier from harbour
   then let him furl his sails in an Avalon bay
   with time to kidnap a dozen *petites sauvages*
   and waft them back to France
   for a few more months of life

   Four days and over Finistère
   this gale may be shrieking
   or storm the cliffs of Mohér
   and claw next week the Skerrymore light
   or the empty Flannans
   reeling to scatter the gannets
   along the Butt of Lewis
   sweeping Cape Wrath and Hoy
   and booming the caves in Papa Stour

Racing now over St. John's tombs
and the fading glow in its patched heart
the Wind gyres into streets overlying
the footpath Sir Humphrey Gilbert took
for his last walk on land
It shakes the seaward shacks of the poor
and shifts to behead the last flowers
on the lawns of the darkened campus
In these gyrations the sea too is locked
and conspires with the sun
that set the lot of us twirling
   to fill this air with warmth and water

and loose its force
next month on the crags of Sumbo
or leap in the ancient fury of levelling
to inch the humps of Lofoten
back to the seafloor

Tonight in a rift of the racing clouds
stars for a moment flicker
over pre-Cambrian cliffs that shelter now
the cocktail lounge of the Pink Poodle
See where a satellite creeps
in this cloudgap   whispering perhaps
in private to lonely towers and tossing freighters
whatever the tale of tempests to come
    whispering till it too is pulled down
    somewhere by the earth's weight
    to burn into dust for the Wind
squalling now on Cape Spear and into these toy
galleons dancing

    the Wind that will go bellowing
    over Cape Farewell and frosted Nordkapp
    the captious Wind that drowned Chancellor
    and spared Ottar a millennium back
    to tell King Alfred the first tale
    of great whales and walrus waiting
    to die that men might be rich

    Beyond Novaya Zembla
    beyond the pack-ice in the Laptev Sea
    the Wind will sweep
    as it swept over Bering's bones on Wrangel
    and skimmed the polar ice to Amundsen's Gulf

 polishing Hearne's name on a Coppermine rock
and come again declaiming through a St. John's town

saying only that air and earth and sea will be one
and whirl in the Sun
within the reeling Circle

Newfoundland, 1977

BIRTHDAY

Some nine hundred fifty circlings of my moon
i doubt i'll see a thousand
my face lunar with wrinkles
the strings of my limbs unravelling
trunk weak at the core as an old elm's

worse   the brain's chemistry out of kilter
memory a frayed net
speech a slowing disc the needle jumps

& yet i limp about   insist in fact
on thanking the sky's pale dolphin
for flushing & plumping herself once more
into a pumpkin—
that storybook Moon still in my child mind
too deep for any astronaut to dig out

& stubbornly i praise the Enormous Twist
that set my sun to spinning me
these 26,663 times on the only known planet
that could sprout me

i praise too the great god Luck
that grew me into health
(out of mumps, chicken pox, measles, pneumonia,
                                    scarlet
fever, diphtheria, enteritis, & a dozen broken bones)
Luck that freed me to roam & write
and gave me a lifetime of friends

some dawns it's true came up with betrayal
or failure   rejection   bombs dropping
they taught me only happiness had been
& could be again .

Sophocles said it's better not to be born
but he waited till 90 to tell us
at 74 i'm too young to know

so i bless whatever stars
gave me a cheerful father
with a bold heart & a dancing body
who passed me his quick eye & ear
& his faithful love-affair with words

& how can i not be grateful
to a Universe that made
my most enduring mother?
she too valued Luck   but she bet on Pluck
If ever deed of mine achieved
a glint of the unselfish
it was a fallen spark
from her lifetime's fire

when i give my dust to the wind
it will be with honest thanks
to those fellow earthlings
who forgave or forgot
my onetime alongtime suffering wife
our brilliant son   his loving enduring mate
& those handsome grandsons they brought us
& to those comrades who held me
steady on cliffs

above all my gratitude
to whatever Is above all
for the young who light my evening sky
& for Her   my happiest Happenstance
if She remember me with love
when She is old
it will be immortality enough

May 1978

the sun never sets
it is we who rise
& think
to shine

1983

WANDERVÖGEL

I go on the gobus the gosub the gotrain
and sit by a magic electrickle window
    that protects while i'm gazing so cool
on the indigo flowers that zoom up from plants
    where nobody plants any more

i am stirred by the dramas of gods unseeing
who breathe my oxygen in while exhaling
    essence of verjuice and making
vinegar lakes a fixture at last
    but keeping me upright and movable

while wagnerian chariots are roaring around me
carloads of carclones are coming to swaddle
    the roads of my city in all
the unbreathable perfumes while pyramids also
    of sawdust my window reveals

the flayed flesh of the fresh-air-makers
who died that others like me might still
    be almost alive and gliding
on these necromantical wheels to where
    with a great magnavoxical voice

i'll recite to a soundproofed roomfull of scholiards
safe from the decibellations of stelco
    and o'keefe's brewery this pome

and be speeded back through identical steelways
in time to catch before dinner

on tv

Via Rail, 1982

"There is no no"

There is no no
and never is ever
for time is a pointless
point that ticks us
back from tomorrow's
joy to the yes
of woe and the ceaseless
now

1986

th seekurt ov my fan
tastik sukses az a po
tree reedr iz my pomez havn
nenny hewmur so weneye giv reednz
evribawdee noze
eyem nawt treyen no funni biznes
inennee kase gaffawzer daynjerus
peepul huv gawnintuh con
vulshuns uv glee an dyed
laffn at layton enwen purr
dee reeds wimmin hav
split theyr sides n bin
rush tah hospital n expyred
in stitchez so ime awlwuz kairful
tuhbee dedlee seereeus   that way
no wunz goan ta soo
me fer rekless rye thing
withowta lie sense beekaws
nobuddy ever gotta rest
id fer boarinna oddee ens
ta deth

url burley

Explorers say that harebells rise
from the cracks of Ellesmereland
and cod swim fat beneath the ice
that grinds its meagre sands
No man is settled on that coast
The harebells are alone
Nor is there talk of making man
from ice cod bell or stone

1952

And now in Ellesmereland there sits
a town of twenty men
They guard the floes that reach to the Pole
a hundred leagues and ten
The warders watch the sky watch them
the stricken hills eye both
A mountie visits twice a year
And there is talk of growth

1965

At last in Ellesmereland's hotels
for a hundred fifty each per night
we tourists shit down plastic wells
and watch tv by satellite
The "land beyond the human eye"
the Inuit call it still . . .
Under the blinding midnight sky
subs and missiles wait our will

1985

CANADA: CASE HISTORY: 1945

This is the case of a high-school land,
dead-set in adolescence;
loud treble laughs and sudden fists,
bright cheeks, the gangling presence.
This boy is wonderful at sports
and physically quite healthy;
he's taken to church on Sunday still
and keeps his prurience stealthy.
He doesn't like books, except about bears,
collects new coins and model planes,
and never refuses a dare.
His Uncle spoils him with candy, of course,
yet shouts him down when he talks at table.
You will note he's got some of his French mother's looks,
though he's not so witty and no more stable.
He's really much more like his father and yet
if you say so he'll pull a great face.
He wants to be different from everyone else
and daydreams of winning the global race.
Parents unmarried and living abroad,
relatives keen to bag the estate,
schizophrenia not excluded,
will he learn to grow up before it's too late?

Ottawa

CANADA: CASE HISTORY: 1973

No more the high-school land
dead-set in loutishness
This cat's turned cool
the gangling's gone
guffaws are for the peasants

Inside his plastic igloo now
he watches gooks and yankees bleed
in colour on the telly
But under a faded Carnaby shirt
ulcers knife the rounding belly

Hung up on rye and nicotine and sex-
y flicks, kept off the snow and grass
he teeters tiptoe on his arctic roof
(ten brittle legs, no two together)
baring his royal canadian ass
white and helpless in the global winds

Schizoid from birth, and still a sado-masochist
this turkey thinks that for his sins
he should be carved while still alive:
legs to Québec, the future Vietnam;
the rest, self-served and pre-digested,
to make a Harvest Home for Uncle Sam . . . .

Teeth shot and memory going
(except for childhood grudges),
one moment murderous, the next depressed,

this youth, we fear, has moved from adolescence
into what looks like permanent senescence.

Toronto 1973

[File Update] This is now no high-school land
Adult & schizoid he admits to thinking sometimes
he is the Third World's Saviour.
But then his mood will swing
from euphoria to complainings
(oil is leaking from his arctic roof).
Depression triggers nightmares:
he is a tightrope clown
but with ten brittle legs no two in step.
"Or," he says shyly, "I'm in my Mountie uniform
but my pants have slipped.
I'm standing bare-assed in the arctic winds."
Given Rorschach he found a turkey
. . . decapodal . . . which he would carve alive.
"Drumsticks," says he, "I'd promise to the West.
Wings to the Atlantic; Ontario the neck,
giblets for the tundra, breast to Québec.
But first I'd pass the platters down to Uncle.
He has the cutlery. And anyway
it's his Thanksgiving Day
we really keep."

FYTTE THE HINDMOST

for Wailan

BEGINNING

the miracle leaps
in the sap unseen
under the scarred elm's bark
to a skyfull of buds

the truth runs
from the old
hands on the keys
to the song in the young throat

the magic flows
in the wind that bends
the waterlily's face
to the lips of the wrinkling lake

Uxbridge 1973/1985

SHE IS

for wailan, on her 24th birthday

she is
a little spruce tree
fresh every way
herself
like a dawn

when warm winds come
she will move
all her body
in a tremble of light

but today she stands
in magical stillness
she has clasped
all my falling flakes
from the round of her sky
and wished them
into her own
snowtree

through the cold time
she holds me
with evergreen
devotion
she bears up my whiteness

o so light may i press
letting each needle

grow in her own
symmetry
for i am at peace
in her form
after whirling
and faithful to all
her curves

but when warm winds come
we must stir from this trance
she will lift living arms
to the sun's dance

i will slide then
in a soft caress
of her brown sides
and my falling will end
somewhere in her roots

may my waters then
bring her strength only
help her hold trim
and evergreen her being
with suns and winds
for o many and many
and happiest years

Treehouse, Uxbridge 1974

some mornings trying to write
i get like an old ruffed partridge
flopping off & on the nest
scared somebody'll steal
those handsome brown eggs
i've never quite laid yet

flinching from cloud shadows
hearing a fox behind every bush
snakes in the grass
shots on the hill—
limping & trembling around
from what looked like a man
but was only a dumb moose—
till i crumple down beat
with nothing done
& then the phone rings

but listen!
it isn't another mag salesman
or the Poets' League about dues
out of that lovely earpiece
comes a voice spreading sunshine
all through the woods
& i sit back drumming softly
to the loveliest partridge of all
(whose eggs they really are)
& feeling energy-control
right down to my wingtips

after we hang up
quietly i'm warming the eggs again
if i can't lay i can hatch
maybe something of me
will show in the chicks

Alexander St., 1974

an arkfull she is
of undulant creatures
a cinnamon bearcub
curled in a warm ball
thinking of honey & berries
nuts roots or even
grass jelly for supper

a sturdy raccoon too
with masked eyes
& dexterous forepaws
very frequent to bathe
& a bandit of ice cream
who sleeps a lot
with one soft hindpaw
poking most modestly out

or a shy bobcat
coloured olive-brown
or maybe pale gold
with round
slipper-fur feet
on which she sits very quiet
and so thoughtful
beside her leafy plants
she is sometimes invisible
though very much there

she can be an ochre
squirrel as well
sinuous & all compact

alert & frisky
& away & back like a dream
& whatever creature
she is its peaceful emissary
most faithful
& most loving

Toronto 1974

a new city bus she is too
neat & with her own
not always predictable
route to travel

it's a pleasure just to wait
peer up the street
& here she comes
nimble & quick
but caring for kids
& polite to trucks

with small sneezes she stops
& glides me away
the only passenger
while the people outside
fall silent & take on colour
she has put them on tv
with the sound off
now nothing needs to be understood
& anyone might be a hero

behind the clear round
of her windows
through a still possible world
she carries me loving
& safe in herself

Davisville Ave., 1975

from the dark pit
hand firm in hand
we walk up a sunfilled slope
the strange flowers above
bless us and beckon
escaped from time past
we are seven now both
i too am chinese
our obsidian eyes are bright
the fresh-peeled nectarines
in our cheeks

there is no need to talk
we know we are mounting at last
to our rightful life
waiting over the rim
we hear already the birds in song
we bring from our first world
only the one heart's pacer
we fashioned together

its pulse is lifting us now
to twice ten thousand days
we will have time at last
to become and beget
before fading
still loving
as one

i wake
and return to this vision

feeling our linked hands
more certain than all existence
this dream from desire is lava-deep
i cannot believe death's cold crater
will contain it

Scarborough Hospital, July 1975

At six you folded paper boats
with nowhere to sail them down
except a tub in Chinatown

Sixteen you climbed into a dory
to heave through sloughs of English Lit
and came by a dying lake to sit

Then we shaped our own canoe
birch-delicate but strong
and big enough for two

Over the portage freed
we steer through rapids worth the battling
They flow to a living sea

Sit straight dear twenty-six
hold firm the blade you've made
Mine dips with yours however frayed

With luck and will we'll reach
at last some bronzed arbutus beach
From there you'll sail the world

Give my old paddle then a simple burning
Sift the ashes down
where the fish and weed are turning

    But today   sweet twenty-six
    rest your eyes from the current's shine

loose your small palms from the coursing
let them find mine.

January, 1976

Your voice abstracts in a telephone
from melody to monotone
while me the instrument allows
only grunts and male meows
I need your eyes to shine my love on
This doesnt have your melon smell on
I want to squeeze real flesh and bone
unloosed from the clutch of a telephone.

Balliol St., 1976

FUSION

no welding
of ores or floes
no liquation
of salt pillars
no sunthaw of drift
deliquescence of hardness
is like the melding
wherever my bones
fuse & dissolve
in your soft body
& we sleep into one
twinned
& twined
till we wake

and rise
still
welded

Toronto, March 1976

NEVER BLUSH TO DREAM

*to a melody in the "Chrysanthemum Rag" of
Scott Joplin*

I

never blush to dream
a lost love
slides into your bed again

there's no treason
though the blood stirs
when a stranger speaks his name

    each lover keeps the home
    he made within your mind
    and has a key
    to lie with you unbidden
    so long as you are holding
    gentle thoughts of him

2

never feel a guilt
to hear me
whisper still within the night

old loves lurk in eyes
that brighten
to the new enchanter's sight

i too must rise from warmth
to drift with other ghosts
from worldly view
yet i'll come into your bed
some night again
and dream myself alive in you

Toronto, 1977

i'm going to be real mad
if it dies
    wailan sprays briskly
    the potted rosebush
    she womanhandled back to our flat
    a crimson cloud for easter

we wont let it
    i say firmly
    but puzzled what alchemy
    the local plantshop used
    to trick this rambler
    into april resurrection

    wailan does not wonder
    being twenty-seven she believes
    i can keep the sap alive
    even at seventy-two

    after three days
    the blossoms wreathe our floor

April 1977

the flat's not real
a room restored
in a period museum
exact but unconvincing
i do not believe the tv
will turn on

your small slippers
poke from under the chesterfield
something arranged
by a slick director
they do not move
lacking the brown feet
which were human
with minute calluses

i water the chrysanthemum
silent as a photograph
nothing drinks
the armchair
stiff with air

only the bed
grows & is heard
twice as big
petrified with tousling
& yet an imitation too
a stuffed animal

nothing warm under the fur
no
body

July 1977

You'll find my Princess wintertime
bogged down in a swamp at York
but come summer she'll be singing
somewhere in grass by a waterside
Cwowk corse cwowk course i said "singing"
she never croaks   like me
man she's a Princess
Rana pipiens   the meadow frog

Our very first night she sang me
the oldest Batrachian folksong
made music high and true
just for this lanky bullfrog
me   *Rana clamitans*

You probably think she's a green thing
to live with a wrinkled croaker like me
but *lawks* no she's pale brown
it's those crickety treefrogs are green
the chaps that go *qurrrrk qurrrrakk*
like a thumbnail over a comb
The Princess is beige and smooth
as an Anjou pear   pear without spot

Kwawtt what?   Me sing?   *Alawk* no
it's like those biologists say
"bullfrogs utter bass croaks and moans
though sometimes a piercing cry"
Yeah maybe i look pretty silly
hopping around on my big flat feet

the jowls on my belly quivering
though most times i'm sitting quiet
but busy   flip-flick   flip-flick
lassoing every bug in sight

There ought to be statues to frogs
We're the best friends of Man
of Dogs too   all you hot-blooded fellows
We kill fleas flies gnats gnits
bugs mosquitoes no-see-ums
we're insecticidal maniacs
and no DDT needed

Kwowkh kwatt? "Venomous!" Us?!
You've got us mixed with our distant cousins
way off at Toad Hall
and even they aren't "venomous"
they won't give you warts
just a blister or two
though they've sure got enough to give away
Some toads are all wart
Still they're okay in a lumpish way
They flick a neat bug too
but not of course with our speed and finesse
Kwort kwort? I haven't got worts—
well one or two tiny ones
spawts more like
& the princess has absolutely none

Sure we think we're appealing

kwexy-wexy as we say
& we're known to be quite amorous
"A Frog he would a-wooing go, heigh ho!"

97

They don't sing that about toads
And what do those Greek frogs croak
when they make up a chorus?
Brek-ke-kek-kek ko-ax ko-ax
They're still singing it by the ponds in Crete
Sounds real sexy to me
the same they performed for Aristophanes
two thousand years and more ago
You don't believe me read his *Frogs*
a whole play about our Greek connection
Brek-ke-kek-kex the boys at Harvard
chant it still at ball games *ax* anybody

Krek-kroax krockle-chuckle   that's me now
& i can do *krowg-jowg jowg-krom*
jowg-o-rum   more rum!
that's pretty bacchanalian eh?

Ah but you must wait
till the Princess comes back
if you want to hear my piercing cry

1978

Sometimes when i'm the one
away from pond
i get feeling so insecure
i worry even about Mr. Toad

& that's a laugh
how could a bullfrog like me
lose his Princess to a toad?
We all know about toads i hope
how they're not a patch on frogs
can't sing a note
or swim worth a damsite
Sometimes they'll sit on the bottom of a swamp
just to show they're amphibians too
but mostly they squat in grubby corners
whereas we're the athletes of the Two Worlds
Frogs were holding Batrachiads
before lungs even
hop-and-skip or broad
In our weight class we swim faster
than East Germans
Why we invented the breaststroke
(you should see the Princess
a skinny-dipping beauty)
As for jumping
that old-timer in Calaveras County
whom Mark Twain said he coached
gets his record broken every year
Frogs never needed coaching
we'll jump yards just for the hell of it
But nobody's ever heard of a jumping toad.

So how could i be jealous of one?
Well it's this way:
the Princess & i feel sorry for toads
they're retarded but they're our kinfolk

So we run a benevolent society
the Toad Lovers' Club
& keep a kind of heraldic figure
a Totem Toad in our bedroom
He sits between our pillows

O he's just stuffed of course
with batten or something   plastic eyes
but they're very big & wistful
& his hide's real velvety & green
more like a frog's
except he's dumb & helpless
just sits there waiting for us

Or is it just for the Princess?
That's what i ask myself now i'm away

Still even Othello
& he was a real jealous type
wasn't suspicious of toads
In fact he thought they had no appetite
for anything   just brooded in wells
lived off vapour
no yen for love like us frogs

But Milton now he was more wary
thought there was a toad in Eden
"close at the ear of Eve"
& up to no good
Makes me wonder what people mean

when they say "toads complete a garden"
That toad was an agent for the Snake

Sure sure ours isn't real
an imaginary toad
but he's in a real Garden
& it's reserved for the Princess & me

I tell myself if Mr. Toad wasn't beside her
who knows what young pipsqueak *pipiens*
elegantly slim & amber-eyed
wouldn't be leaping around that pillow
spellbinding my Princess with his frogsong

I'm going to hop the next plane home

1978

4 p.m.
moon's umbrage slides over Sun
we are a lozenge in His mouth
the owl has hushed
light dries
chills
only the other suns flare out
strange shadows are rippling
over the birch trunks
and sudden fireflies around the porch
are coldly dancing

i see my love 5000 kilometres away
walking in the noonday Sun
wordless i feel her lips
move into mine

September, 1977

MOMENT OF ECLIPSE (2)

four on a summer's afternoon
suddenly the moon
slides over our Sun
and we are a lozenge in her mouth

that owl has hushed
light dries   chills
only the other suns
far away flare up . . .

on the birch trunks
without source
a riffle of shadows

around our porch
instant fireflies
coldly dancing

i glimpse
my love walking
three thousand miles away
in the noonday Sun

soundless the lips of another
move into hers

1977

DIVING

loving you i hold my breath
i dive from dryness
slide to softer meadows
where all is upsidedownness
silence   yielding
to silence

and then since love
is winged by words
wants air for launching
we heave aloft
are warmed in a glitter of sounds
flaked away by the wind

but loving you is beyond wings
is to dive and dive and
sway with primal weed
is to dance with fins
in a joy too salt
for sounding

1978

LOOKING UP

(for Wailan on her 29th)

love   you draw back
from the sight of maybe 70 more storeys
in the mist above

to stay on this level always
who wouldn't?   house plants everlasting
but the tenancy rule is one UP each year
or OUT

when i had to move to the 29th
i was so desperate i tried to block
the elevator with rejected manifestos

crazy?   we all know almost
nothing in this highrise goes DOWN
not even the stairs
& the management refuses escalators

so ime on the 74th & set to move
UP UP till ime really breathless
& the Super shoves me OUT the chute
with the garbage

but you & i   love
we dont let this bother us
we have our secret fire-escape
to go & come between floors
it lets me sit today beside your lilies
pecking out my certainty

the apartments further UP
will be even better for you
with whatever flatmate

love   let the Landlord worry
about next year's lease

sit with me now & look beyond the geraniums
at this moment's simple sky
in the best of all 29th storeys

Balliol St., January 1979

VALENTINE FOR MS. LUTRIS

I love an otter
a roly-poly sea-otter.
She was born beside the blue Pacific's rim.
There she floated on her fanny
in a manner quite uncanny
that has kept her trolly-roly slim.
She can paw a rock, lorlumme,
and two urchins* to her tummy
and bang the lot together for a dinner.
She's my very special otter,
makes her salads from sea water:
a clam, a mussel, and some kelp for a beginner.

Once her folk, of such distinction,
were murdered almost to extinction
by jerks who only for her furskin sought her.
Now we treasure all sea-otters,
the most chic of ocean's daughters,
while their shining pelts are still upon 'em,
which is why ships never oughter
spill their oil on otters' waters,
also why, dear cuddliest creature of the brine,
Enhydra lubris, O Ms Otter otter,
I beg you, please, to be my VALENTINE.

1979

Urchins? young Homines sapientes?! *No no!* Strongylo-
centroti purpurati, *sea hedgehogs, what the French call*
Oursins, *and the West Coast Indians recognize as* Kwa-
gulth, *sisters.*

a tree-stem
hollowed
8 holes   hidden in 1
is a fipple   a knob
edged to blow breath over
a blockflute

at stonehenge they found one
carved from a ram's bone
(and before that how many centuries
of herd-girls piping?)

held simply in the hands   end-blown
more basic than the wheel
and less pervertible

january 27, 1980
this one in a cardboard box
totally unpretending   like you
holding within
mysteries intangible
melodies climbing by magic intervals
from pastures to cathedrals

i hear your first notes
this birthday morning
one by plaintive one
they have already your gentleness
they strive for precision
yearn for the overtones   persist
toward song

love may the next thirty years
bring you time and recorders
to blow out in bravura
whatever is blocked unshared
misprized within you
and let there always be one
when i am deaf
who hears the music your breath makes
now in me   by merely breathing

Toronto, January 1980

believe this whisper
(even a husk may shape a prophecy)
believe i hear
among the young intrepid bees
that buzz your summer
one that will burst through pollen
singing
there will be berries brightening
before the autumn's burnish
while deep in wintered earth
i meld into your taproot
into the holdfast we made
in our spring

1981

to be alive with you is life enough
for singing any time
to wake beside you on your birthday
is to dance my january back to may

we watch beyond our window the ice-bright maples
cold-shouldering every snowflake
each unique geometry going down
to dissolution in the shapeless drifts

we see   but twined we stay
in love's warm garden on this happy day
this orchard where the flowering peach
fulfills a slip bequeathed from Chang-an's arbors
where poets walked   supped wine   made love
and music through perhaps as many centuries
as years you have today, sweet thirty-two

what? you sigh   some pink petals dropped already?
but that's lucky!   only the fallen float to poems
Li Po stared between such ambiguities to find
his love for Wong Lun all the deeper
   (as mine, Wai Lan, for you)
This mottled leaf the winds of autumn overlooked
   rides still to you

So be up, dear one, and see the clouds roll back
the sun contrive a glory from the spectral city
where we dumbly join the seven deadly dancers
   but not this joyful Day

today we dance to our own tunings
safe in the garden of our Now
that we have grown   and by our embracing
still embraces us

1982

A
soiled mop of
petals in february
grass this heart of
mine is an old dandelion
that survives still by your

I

L
O
V
E

When
all the certified
flowers blazed from the
earth of your spring you
painted them but it was this
rusting weedseed you tended

You fed me courage beyond hope or deserving
and watered my wits. From smothering leaves
you held me free in the fingers of your
patience, shone music, danced my rags
to ragtime, kept my heart beating
with the joy of loving

Y
O
U

14 February 1983

my love is young & i am old
she'll need a new man soon
but still we wake to clip and talk
to laugh as one
to eat and walk
beneath our thirteen-year-old moon

good moon   good sun
that we do love
i pray the world believe me
& never tell me when it's time
that i'm to die
or she's to leave me

Toronto, 1973–1986

AVE ATQUE VALE

Over the hill and
sinking fast in the bog
i've time just to wave

one muddy hand

1986

WHEN WE MUST PART

sweetheart, think that my death
swings wide your harbour's mouth
to welcome in the young and joyful
the quick eyes ready for the searoads
time is yours for choosing
the love to sail the world with

(and the father to make with you
the unborn waiting to be loved)

if clouds hang heavy now
remember how your gentle sun
wheeled my rough planet round you
believe in my belief
that you were made to shine
with love
and being loved

swim proud dear princess
let no one dim
the brilliance of your mind
let no one bind
the courage of your heart

my small one so tall in patience
i think you will grow wise as Orcas
yet never lose your dolphin curves

1977/1986

END

Wailan dearest
in your spring
you took my arm
to walk with me
into my snowscape

You must tramp back now
Summer still waits for you
Make it be long
Let the sun fill it

Then autumn
with pumpkin and mangoes
a fireplace shared
to warm another
with the same love
you shone steadfast on me

If sometime my shadow
flits over the embers
it's just to bless.

1987

A Note on the Text

Last Makings was edited by Marlene Kadar and Sam Solecki. Earle Birney had almost finished rewriting the book before illness prevented any further work. When he submitted the first, incomplete version of *Last Makings* to McClelland & Stewart on August 27th, 1985, it was accompanied by the following letter:

This book is in 2 parts, each arranged in chronological order of writing or of the period of the contents.

A.   45 poems of travel (mainly), of which 9 are here published for the first time, 8 have appeared only in magazines, 15 are reprinted from *Fall by Fury* (because that book is now o.p.). Another 13 poems will be available in a few weeks for this book.

B.   24 poems of love, also arranged chronologically between 1973 and 1985, all addressed to Wailan Low. Of these, 5 are new, one has been published only in a magazine, and 18 are reprinted from *Fall by Fury* or *Ghost in the Wheels*. Many of these have been to some extent revised or reworked.

I am still doubtful if some of these poems are good enough for inclusion—especially the long "Letter to Leonardo." I hope to have your advice on such matters. The title poem is placed last.

EB

The manuscript exists in two versions: the first, and earlier one is in a black binder (MS 1), and many of the poems have changes in Birney's handwriting. The second

(MS 2), a much cleaner typescript, was put together by Wailan Low from the author's papers. Although the same poems appear in both manuscripts, the second or later version of a poem is often quite different from the earlier one. In at least two cases the difference is so great that the editors have chosen to print both ("Lifeboat" and "moment of eclipse"). In instances where it was clear that the first manuscript contained the later version of a poem, the editors chose it instead of the one in the typescript. We also decided to drop the lengthy prose piece, "Letter to Leonardo," which even the author doubted to be "good enough for inclusion."

Some changes in punctuation and spelling were made only after consulting both manuscripts, previously published versions of the poems, and Wailan Low. Some other points of editorial or textual interest are noted below:

"Early Passion in Banff." Only in MS 2.
"Deer Hunt, 1908." Only in MS 1.
"Port Alberni to Grimsby by Limey Freighter, 1934." Birney's notes indicate that he intended to add thirteen poems to this sequence. At the time of his stroke he had written only the titles.
"Seadancers." When the poem was published in *Grain* (Spring 1987), it appeared with this note: " 'Seadancers' began as a prose paragraph in a private 'log' I was keeping in the autumn of 1934. I had shipped as a deckhand on a British freighter, the *Filleigh*, en route from Port Alberni, B.C., to Grimsby on the North Sea coast of England, via the Panama Canal. By the time we got there I had about sixty pages of prose diary and half a dozen pieces of verse. This is the only one of the poems unpublished till now. I hadn't submitted it anywhere because I had a block about the ending, which I didn't

bypass till the autumn of 1986, fifty-two years later."

"Canada to Mexico." Birney's notes to MS 1 indicate that he probably intended this to be a two-part poem with "Letter to Leonardo" (also referred to as "Rambling with Leonardo") as the second part.

"Trawna tuh Belvul by Knayjin Psifik." This is a much shortened version of the poem first published in *Fall by Fury*.

"Canada: Case History: 1945," "Canada: Case History: 1973," and "Canada: Case History: 1985" were inserted by the editors on the assumption that readers might want to read the three poems as a sequence. (The author is responsible for the inclusion of the two earlier "Ellesmereland" poems.)

The author's original table of contents shows that he intended to close "Fytte the Fyrst" with "Remarx" and "For George Johnston." Neither was completed.

Acknowledgements

To the following periodicals which gave earlier publication to many of these poems:

AUSTRALIA
Poetry Australia

CANADA
Acanthus, Antigonish Review, British Columbia Historical Quarterly, Blewointment, Brick, Canadian Forum, Canadian Literature, Descant, Event, Grain, Nebula, New Horizons, Ontario Review, Quarry, Tamarack Review, Toronto Life, Waves

GREAT BRITAIN
Ambit, Envoi, Outposts, Trends

U.S.A.
Atlantic Monthly, Evenfield Review, Happiness Holding Tank, Niagara Magazine, Quartet

Earlier, slightly different versions of some of these poems were also published by McClelland & Stewart in *Fall by Fury*, now out of print, and a few others in *Ghost in the Wheels*.

Printed in Canada